IRON MEN

Forging Gospel Men

NATHAN BLACKABY

CWR

About Nathan

Nathan Blackaby is the Executive Director of CVM (Christian Vision for Men), a global movement of men focused on introducing a million men to Jesus Christ. Nathan leads the team at CVM, speaking to and reaching thousands of men each year with the gospel.

The author of *Founding Fathers* and other CVM resources, Nathan enjoys writing and blogging, and has taken on a few sporting challenges such as cycling in Romania and a triathlon.

Nathan has been married to Jennie for 15 years and together they have three children. He hails from Essex and loves gaming, motorbikes, fast cars and darts.

Contents

Foreword

For the last twenty or so years I've been a biker. Not a hard-core biker whose life is defined by bikes, but someone who uses a bike as a tool to get through the traffic on the daily commute. I reckon on a good day I can save about forty-five minutes on my journey into work – and that's not something to be sniffed at!

But here's the thing about bikes: they're dangerous on many different levels. One lapse of concentration, one car driver who isn't looking, one misjudged corner and you're potentially done for. However, so far I've never been hit by a car or misjudged a corner. In fact, I've never had any form of accident on my motorbike (when it's been moving, but that's another story!). The reason for that is a great instructor, and regularly riding with a group of blokes who swap tips and advice. Biking has a bit of a community attached to it – wherever you go, if you find a fellow biker, once they know you are one of them, they'll take the time to stop and talk. Only the other day in London I saw a man getting onto a brand new Honda Africa Twin (a bike I've been keen to look at), so I popped over the road and told him I had a Honda VFR but was keen to see this new bike. He dropped everything to chat with me enthusiastically, to the point where, 20 minutes later, we were talking generally about riding and swapping ideas on bits of kit. That's the biking community for you – and I love it.

However, as I said, I'm not defined by bikes. I'm defined by Jesus Christ and a decision I made in 1990 to follow Him wholeheartedly for the rest of eternity. My eyes and heart are now fixed on Him and I'm determined to follow Him with all my heart, soul, mind and strength. It's not easy though. Life is a game of ups and downs, and one thing is for sure: staying on the narrow path of following Christ isn't straightforward.

When new motorcyclists first start riding bikes and learn how to lean in to corners, they can often end up planting themselves in a ditch – it's a very common accident. The reason is that they look at what they are trying to avoid rather than looking through the bend. If only they had kept their eyes on the meandering road then they would've avoided heading right into the very thing they were desperate not to smash into. Following Jesus is the same. Jesus describes it as going through a narrow gate and staying on a narrow path. Look away from the narrow path and there are plenty of things that will pull you into a ditch.

This book is about getting men to keep their eyes fixed on the right stuff. Not just so that they can feel good but so that they can be the men they know they ought to be, take the fight to the enemy and see their mates and family members won into the kingdom of God.

I've known Nathan for some years now and he lives what he's written. So you can be assured that this book isn't full of fluff, platitudes or unrealistic 'churchianity'. It's forged in the fire of really living for Jesus Christ and putting Him front and centre. So, let's dig into this stuff and keep each other on the narrow path. Allow God to forge and shape your life and you'll never plant yourself in a ditch.

Carl Beech
President of Christian Vision for Men and UK Director of The Message Trust

Introduction

'as a son with his father he
[Timothy] has served with me in
the work of the gospel.' (Phil. 2:22)

I stumbled across this verse in the Bible recently, and it really got me thinking about how we encourage each other and train each other as men who want to share the gospel with our mates, brothers and more.

One of the impacts of having fewer men in church, combined with a degree of lethargy among us Christian men, is that good Christian mentoring is hard to find. Not only do blokes like me in our thirties need older men to guide us, speak into our lives and build faith, but these men (in their forties, fifties and more) need that too!

As we see the gaps in church where men used to be, the generations of men still pursuing Jesus are feeling the lack of brotherhood and mentoring to sharpen them as gospel operators. Why? Because those fellas around us to sharpen our faith just aren't there anymore, and there needs to be an urgent waking up for us.

I think we have some 'keys' in the Bible that we can digest, chew over and then use to be intentional about building each other up as men who are driven to share the gospel and see Jesus change our nation. Do you want to be part of that? Have you ever looked around and thought, 'What other bloke can I turn to and get alongside to pray with me?' 'Where is the group of guys who seek God together, pray together and really set time aside and even prioritise this stuff?'

What are the keys? Well, I recently went out to Brazil, and while I was there I had a catch up with an old friend called Alves. Alves is in his late sixties. His life was marked with alcohol addiction and he wandered for years in the interior of Brazil, a dry and arid place, looking for something to fill his emptiness. Alves, a homeless man and desperate alcoholic, found something that changed his life: Jesus Christ.

When I worked at Teen Challenge, Alves was part of the leadership team there. Each day he would call me over when I arrived at the centre and show me something new from the Bible – a key that he'd found.

Alves' keys, to be frank, were like a ball and chain around my ankle at first. I tried to avoid him but he would find me. I would try getting there late to see if he had gone already. I would walk in looking into my mobile phone as if I was on the edge of a really important deal that couldn't, under any circumstances, be interrupted, but still he did. It wasn't that I disliked getting the keys from Alves; I guess if I'm honest I thought I knew it all. I was in a way of thinking that didn't want to be taught, wouldn't sit at someone's feet to learn – I was too busy trying to change the world. Sometimes he challenged me and it was uncomfortable; sometimes he had a really specific word from the Holy Spirit and that, too, was often a bit uncomfortable.

However, I gradually realised that I was learning something of great value, both in these moments and about the bigger picture of intentional mentoring and working together for the gospel.

When I was in Brazil again recently I thanked Alves for the investment he had made in my life, and he responded by saying, 'Nathan, each of us has these keys from Scripture that we can read and trust. Then we share them with the men around us and build each other up for working in the field.'

Field? Keys? Is any of this making sense?

Nathan (left) and Alves (right) opening the Bible together in Brazil

Back in the UK I have really missed this. It is so easy to talk about everything and anything rather than opening our Bibles together and digging up some of these keys.

Why are we so reserved about inviting someone we know to explore this stuff? Why do guys my age not seek these men out? Where are they? Are they there? Can we inspire them to share what they have found out about the gospel? Are you one of those men?

I had a beer with three guys recently. All were in their late fifties and sixties. All had been married for over thirty years, and I asked them for something they could share with me about what they had learnt. I asked them to 'give me some keys' to nurturing a healthy marriage.

I received one solid response, lots of blank looks and glazing over, and then something just about themselves as husbands. Sounds harsh but, guys, we need to be ready for this stuff. We need to be able to grasp these keys because generations of men need to hear it.

What are they asking? Let me tell you:

- How can I grow in my faith and boldness to carry the gospel forward?
- How can I impact my family with the truth of Jesus?
- How can I win battles in my private life and social life that will feed my faith in Jesus, and let others see Jesus lives?
- How can I make my family a priority when work is so pressured?

- How can I nurture intimacy with Jesus on a daily basis?
- What has worked for you?
- How did you do it/how are you doing it?

If I asked you what the keys are for winning people to Jesus, what might you say? Would you give me the well-known John 3:16?

Reader, I (probably) don't know you, but maybe you are 55 and need to be mentored. Maybe you are 55 and can see how you can mentor others. Maybe you are 20 and need to look for this sort of support, or maybe you are 20 and can see guys of the next generation who need help to be gospel men, on fire with the good news of Jesus!

This is not about life coaching to build a better 'you', this is about training us to be an elite band of gospel commandos. Men who are pulling the pin on gospel grenades and leading a charge into our homes, workplaces, personal and private lives, churches and communities with the good news of Jesus Christ!

Nor is it intended as a criticism; this comes from a deep longing to see men empowered and show that we have to step up and be a new kind of men. We need to be men who respond to the necessity around us because it is urgent, not only for the older men who need mentoring and need to mentor, but for the waves of younger men who want to learn, and need to seek guidance and direction.

Let me tell you a quick story. On 14 June 1922, at the age of 45, a man called Major Hesketh Hesketh-Prichard died in Gorhambury, Hertfordshire.

The major was born in India and was a big game hunter, explorer, adventurer, writer, cricketer and soldier. When he managed to work his way to the frontline during the First World War (a difficult job as by then he was an older man for military service) he discovered something, born from necessity.

Under sporadic sniper fire from German soldiers dug into strategic positions, Major Hesketh Hesketh-Prichard realised that his ability with his scoped hunting rifle was birthing a new form of combat. At that point the military had no official sniping and scouting regiment, but they did after the Major had arrived. Out of necessity came a response, strategic, focused and intentional – The 1st Army School of Scouting, Observation and Sniping.

We can respond to the necessity around us to intentionally train focused gospel men, who have in their possession the keys of faith discovered in the Bible. These men pass on this training, they inspire and equip one another and together make an incredible move forward to win more men for Jesus Christ.

This book has been written with my Bible open in front of me at 1 and 2 Timothy. Paul's gospel investment into Timothy's life is incredible. Perhaps before you read on, go and look at 1 and 2 Timothy for yourself.

Then go and get a cuppa.

Part 1

Let's build

1. Foundations

'when I call to remembrance the
genuine faith that is in you, which
dwelt first in your grandmother
Lois and your mother Eunice'
(2 Tim. 1:5, NKJV)

So let's kick this off, but perhaps from a slightly different starting point than you might expect: building foundations!

In the Bible, Paul makes it clear that faith stuff was part of the family that Timothy was born into. It looks like Timothy's nanna Lois found her faith in Jesus, and then his mother Eunice did too.

These two women set about teaching young Timothy about Jesus, opening the Scriptures with him. The Bible tells us that right from his childhood, Timothy was shown the truth, so that when he met Jesus for himself he was ready to make the right choice.

What's this got to do with mentoring and building up gospel men with a heart and passion for Jesus? Well, I think this building of foundations is so important, primarily in the home.

I've got a son and two daughters and they are my primary arena for mentoring and spiritual formation. My wife and I have been given the job and honour of opening the Bible with our children and helping them know about Jesus. They will need to meet Him for themselves and make a choice to follow Him or not, but like Lois and Eunice, the ground must be prepared.

You might not have had that sort of background at all, and the fella you are being mentored by or whom you are mentoring might not have had that sort of upbringing either. No problem. What is important here is that we see the foundation, or empty space and start to build one there.

When I worked for a mate of mine, there was one job I detested. Digging. He would put a spade in my hand, point me towards a marked patch on someone's lawn and I was told to dig. So dig is what I did. We had to lay foundations to build anything; the higher the building or structure was going to be, the deeper the foundation had to be.

The problem was that I couldn't see what the end result was going to look like – I just saw a horrible trench to dig, cutting through thick clay and tree roots. In some cases, when the building already had a foundation, we had to underpin what was already there, basically digging underneath the old foundation to put a new one in – a proper one fit for the job.

However you want to look at this, get a foundation in, and that, my friends, is the truth that Jesus has set you free. You are a new man because of one thing: the blood Jesus shed for you on the cross has dealt with all – yep, *all* – of your sin. Make that truth your foundation and let's start to build.

 Prayer-action

Prayers are not passive. Not only does it take action for us to be honest with God about what's going on in our lives and ask for His help, but God takes action through our prayers – and we are called to action as well. Spend some time talking to Jesus about the foundations you've had. Thank Him for them, or invite Him and His victory at the cross to be your underpinning. Be honest and real with Jesus about who you are and ask Him to show you who He is.

2. Long term

'Let no one despise your youth,
but be an example to the
believers in word, in conduct,
in love, in spirit, in faith, in purity.'
(1 Tim. 4:12, NKJV)

At CVM we have often talked about how long it can take to win a bloke to Jesus. I spoke about Jesus at a recent story café event, and about how, when we talk to one of our mates about Jesus, it can take about five years for him to really see and respond. During this time that mate will need to hear the same gospel about thirty times.

When I had finished speaking, a young guy with a shaved head and piercing eyes that had seen a lot of life shouted out, 'Yes, mate – spot on! It was five years to the day when I gave my life to Jesus – five years since my mate first told me about Jesus.'

Of course, it is not always like that, but that's often what we see. What's the point? Long term is the point.

Timothy was estimated to be in his thirties, pastoring the church in a place called Ephesus, when his mentor Paul wrote him this letter to encourage him. The interesting thing is that this letter comes after about fifteen years of friendship and working together, with Paul intentionally shaping and building Timothy up as a gospel man.

This was a long-term investment, not a quick six-week intensive course. And not only was this a long-term investment, but there were also some long-term goals and targets being put in place and worked towards.

The goals and targets were to be an example:

- In word
- In conduct
- In love
- In spirit
- In faith
- In purity.

So it's actually a pretty big deal being asked here, guys. In your relationships of accountability and mentoring, as you are forging gospel men, what do these areas look like? Are you being made into this sort of man too?

This is about a long-term vision to build gospel men who are a living example in what they say, how they behave,

Jesus lived this

and how they show and act with love. These men will know the Holy Spirit and how He has equipped them; they will manoeuevre bold faith moves and, in public or private, walk with purity honed like granite.

As I write this I am getting fired up – I want to be that sort of bloke. I want to help other fellas be that type of Christian man too. This is not a new message: Jesus lived this, and when He went to glory He sent the Holy Spirit to help us follow in His footsteps.

 ## Prayer-action

Long term, are you ready for this? Spend some time talking to Jesus about who you really want to be, and who you can encourage over the years to come. If this has resonated with you then turn it into prayer fuel, and invite Jesus to put life into it.

3. Journey together

'You, however, know all about
my teaching, my way of life,
my purpose, faith, patience,
love, endurance, persecutions,
sufferings – what kinds of
things happened to me in
Antioch, Iconium and Lystra, the
persecutions I endured. Yet the
Lord rescued me from all of them.'
(2 Tim. 3:10-11)

On one occasion I shared the CVM vision for winning men
with a group of guys in Chester and someone raised the
question, 'How do I do this gospel men stuff when I am so
busy anyway?'

Two answers were given. The first was: busy doing what?
That's not an aggressive challenge; I can busy myself with
101 things that, if I am honest, won't ever make an impact
in my life or an investment in anybody else's.

Secondly I shared how, during my time working in Brazil, I came to experience the work of 'journeying together'. Basically, the conversation went like this: 'I'm going to the tip then I need to pop to the bank, grab a pasty, then head back. Come with me, we can chat.' Obviously I have translated this and made it contextually relevant for the UK, but it was essentially that.

The point I am trying to make is that a crucial element in our being trained as gospel men is journeying together. Invite mates to go where you go, to spend time doing what you do. It's a simple way to not try to programme in yet another meeting or 'thing' to get done – it's far more relational than that.

We have an intern here at CVM and he will come on trips with us, walk to the shop with me, travel in my car with me. Why? So I can intentionally invest in his life, share 'keys' with him, help to forge him as a gospel man. The truth is that, as the guy doing the mentoring, I get a load of stuff back too! In the honest questions I am being asked, the decisions and choices I have made as a Christian are all opened up, processed and explored. It's brilliant!

a crucial element...
is journeying
together

In the Bible, Paul wasn't much different with Timothy. His reason for the journey was to share the gospel and build a foundation on which church communities could be built. Paul led Timothy to faith when he visited Timothy's town. He then went back and invited him to come with him, to journey together. They went to Berea, Athens, Corinth, Jerusalem, Rome and elsewhere.

Did they talk along the journey? You bet they did! Did Paul challenge Timothy, pray with him, and help him to build on this long-term forging of a gospel man? Yep.

If we are to become these gospel men who boldly and unashamedly advance forward with the good news of Jesus, we need to do a bit of journeying together.

Timothy knew Paul; he had seen him without the veneer, he knew he was the real deal. This is also a call and an example for you and me.

 Prayer-action

Speak to Jesus about your life. Ask Him to help you walk the walk, to really live this faith without a veneer. Ask Jesus to help you know how to prioritise this stuff in your life and how to walk with others on this journey.

4. Pass it on

'I hope in the Lord Jesus to send
Timothy to you soon, that I also
may be cheered when I receive
news about you. I have no one
else like him, who will show
genuine concern for your welfare.
For everyone looks out for their
own interests, not those of Jesus
Christ. But you know that Timothy
has proved himself, because as a
son with his father he has served
with me in the work of the gospel.
I hope, therefore, to send him as
soon as I see how things go with
me.' (Phil. 2:19–23)

Here is the reason I am writing this: it's about a baton that is
passed on, a legacy and work that will live beyond you and
me and what we have managed to achieve in our short time.

Paul was in prison in Rome when he wrote this letter. He did later get released and could have visited this church himself, but what is important here is deputisation.

I remember leading a team out to an orphanage in Brazil once. We worked hard, and with the local Brazilian Christian guys we spent a few days painting a concrete football pitch. We spent loads of money on paint and all the kit to do it. We prepped the walls and tasked all the team. The Brazilian guys slowly followed our lead and we worked together on the huge flag murals, one at each end of the pitch.

After a particularly hot day, we had finished resurfacing and painting the floor and just one line was left to do – the centre line across the middle.

One of the Brazilian guys who had worked with us the whole time asked if he could do the final line – the last piece of this epic work of art. I hesitated as I really didn't want him to do it, but I deputised him and gave him the reins. We had worked for this together and it was right that he should take over and lead the way. The line was like a banana that curved from the start point, had a wobble in the middle, then ended up somewhere on the other side.

The outcome was a shame. Out of the whole pitch, that one line burned itself into my dreams, but I am over it now… honest! The lesson I learnt was that we invest in those around us; we train, we guide and empower, but a time will come to hand over the white-line-making machine. The results may not be quite up to your standard

A day will come when they will step forward

or exactly how you wanted them to be, but we must pass on that baton. Later that day we got all the lads out there playing football and they loved it. I sat looking at the line…

The picture Paul uses here is even more dramatic – that of a father and son. I am shaping my son (and my daughters) to be stronger than me, to carry our family name better than I did, to make the choices I couldn't or didn't. A day will come when they will step forward and I will step back. This is essential so keep it in your heart, in your fight to shape and forge gospel men.

Who are you investing in? Who is investing in you? Church leaders, how much time and resources do you spend building this up in your church or ministry? If there is a blank answer to some of these questions at the moment, pray about it because you are not alone. The more we shout about this challenge, the more change we will see.

 **Prayer-action**

Seek Jesus and ask Him to give you a renewed vision. Invite Him to put lives around you and to give you the strength to invest in and deputise these men. Call to Jesus and ask Him to forge in you a wide vision for the gospel men in your circles who are ready to step forward. Invite Jesus to lead you to the fellas who will invest in your next steps.

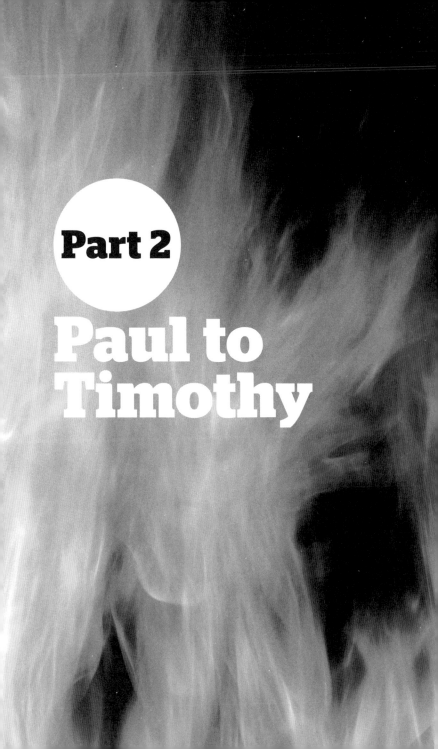

Part 2

Paul to Timothy

1. Love

'The goal of this command is love,
which comes from a pure heart
and a good conscience and a
sincere faith.' (1 Tim. 1:5)

Part of being mentored and mentoring others is about being able to cut through all the rubbish and be honest with each other. If I am being a muppet and need clear guidance then I have people in place to tell me.

Yes, it hurts when I am off track and someone is there to speak the truth. Correction and challenge like that tends to sting no matter what. However, the important thing about it is that we stand again and that it is done because of a relationship that is based on love.

Remember the verse I quoted at the start of the book? (Have a look at Phil. 2:22 in a Bible version of your choice.) Like a father and son! Don't think of this mentoring thing as a once-a-month, formal chat where you take notes and set goals and targets (that might happen, but this is more than that).

I had to correct my son the other day. It was nothing major but it wasn't easy for him to hear. He struggled with it, wrestled with it, but at the end of the day we had both taken a step forward because of it. He sat on his bed and opened his heart to me about other stuff he was holding on to. At just six years old he was confiding in me, being sharpened, and we embraced – a moment that marked me too. Mentoring like this takes on a whole new meaning when we are forging each other with confidence in the gospel.

It's not only the stuff we get wrong that hurts when it gets challenged; sometimes speaking truth and goodness to each other can hurt as well. Seeing that the bloke you are mentoring is gifted in a way that they have battled to really believe, is difficult but essential stuff.

Today's Bible reading is an interesting one, because Paul is telling Timothy to teach and 'charge' some of the guys to only teach the true gospel that they had been given. At that time, some of them had just lost sight of the gospel and begun influencing others with different teaching.

all of this is based on love

The weight behind the word 'charge' is like a military command, or an order. Timothy was to ensure that these guys were all on the same page, and he needed to deal with them – not an easy task.

Paul reminds Timothy that all of this is based on love and that love is the ultimate goal; not doing anything out of hatred or a desire to destroy, but to build. Paul's heart was for the gospel to be seen and heard no matter what. Timothy, a young man, had to call it out, to deal with this stuff, and maybe we need a bit of that too. We need encouragement to speak the gospel, and to look for opportunities to share Jesus. It is often easy to water it down a bit and avoid the moment of saying, 'This is Jesus and what He has done.'

 Prayer-action

As we forge one another into committed gospel men, be ready to be honest with each other; to stay true to the good news message that has set us free. Pray about keeping your sight set right and if you need some recalibration, ask God to help you.

2. Law – Knowing the Word and the Spirit

'Some have departed from these and have turned to meaningless talk. They want to be teachers of the law, but they do not know what they are talking about or what they so confidently affirm.'
(1 Tim. 1:6-7)

At school I was always the kid who could talk his way out of anything. My mouth worked fast and would normally get me out of trouble. I discovered as I travelled around speaking and sharing the vision of CVM that I had a repertoire of funny stories and one-liners that got the laughs and entertained.

But I knew something was not right, because I could go somewhere and share my funny stories but blokes didn't get saved. Entertained maybe, but not saved. Inspired maybe, and encouraged, but not saved. Now this is good stuff and part of the way we share Jesus is through our lives and stories, whether they're funny or not.

However, when the Holy Spirit and the Bible come together, stuff happens and lives get changed. I remember one time when I was on a train to a CVM Glasgow event. I had a talk planned, and I was praying on the journey there. I was moved to pray that God would save one man at the event that day and I felt God say in my spirit, 'Tell them about Jesus then.' So I changed my talk and told them about Jesus, and one bloke made a decision to follow Him.

I realised that the gospel wasn't always being put front and centre, and it needs to be. In this passage about the law, Paul builds on what we looked at previously and encourages Timothy to keep the main thing, the main thing.

Salvation is a free gift; it doesn't need to be added to or have conditions placed around it, which is what the people Paul was writing about were trying to do. They wanted to add a load of proviso and turn salvation into something that works can earn – no good at all!

This got me thinking… We can know *about* the Bible – we can thumb our way to endless verses – but we can actually not really *know* it at all. We can quote it and stick fridge magnets up with Bible verses on them, but not live under the influence of what it is teaching us.

The crowd that Timothy was amongst, and Paul was mentoring Timothy about, wanted to teach and guide people but didn't even know the truth for themselves. They didn't

stuff happens and lives get changed

understand the things they wanted to affirm and teach. It's as if they knew – but they didn't *really* know.

As we mentor others to be these gospel men, soul winners with an unquenchable passion for the lost, we need to realise something: the gospel works. Keep it front and centre. Encourage with it, teach with it, build with it and let the truth of the Bible and God the Holy Spirit set it on fire in the hearts of men.

Prayer-action

**Invite Jesus to refine your vision
of the gospel; to broaden in
your mind the gospel's reach,
power and authority. Invite Him
to forge in you a deep call to
be a gospel man, unafraid, on
fire and released for battle.**

3. Knowing God and His attributes

'Now to the King eternal, immortal, invisible, the only God, be honour and glory for ever and ever. Amen.' (1 Tim. 1:17)

A while ago I went to Bible College. As a bit of a 'failure' at school I was a little nervous about wrestling with concepts and theologies. At the time of my interview I was labouring on a building site and had the day off to attend. In the interview, a wonderful Sri Lankan teacher called Sam said to me, 'Nathan, we do not build houses here; we write essays. Can you do this?'

Well, it was a tough three years and I went to every lecture with an extra notepad to write down all the words I had never heard of. 'Doxology' was one of them. It's just not something you hear while playing darts at the pub, is it? 'Mate, nice shot! By the way, how's your doxology looking?'

In the verses before this one, Paul talks about how God has saved him. Specifically that God has saved him in order

he just pointed back to Jesus

to show others the life that can be found in Jesus. Then Paul does something he does all through the New Testament: he uses these doxologies.

Basically, it's like Paul saying, 'Hey, just so you know, God is totally amazing, awesome and sovereign in all we do.' This is what a doxology is. It's a formalised way of just pointing everything back to God and taking nothing for ourselves.

Paul could have been a bloke who gathered a little bit of glory for himself. He had been beaten up and almost killed for his faith, shipwrecked and chased around because of his belief in Jesus. He didn't ever take the glory, he just pointed back to Jesus.

What these doxologies do is help us come back to God, and know His attributes, promises and complete authority. Paul talks about God as eternal, immortal and invisible. Honour and glory go to God, and that is awesome.

I love watching TV shows set during the medieval age, where Vikings and other cultures of the era carve up land and spoils in a fight for survival. Of course this isn't for everyone, and that's cool. But in these dramas, they stand together and in their own way shout out things like, 'And now to the king!' or, 'Now to the skill of the warrior's hand!'

I like this, and we can do it as we mentor a generation of gospel men.

We can declare who God is together. We can have these doxologies, these 'now to the king' moments together. It keeps our eyes on Jesus, our King and Lord. It keeps our hearts soft to respond when the King speaks, and it keeps the glory going to Him.

Prayer-action

Pray the following prayer and put it into practice in your life: *Now to Jesus, who is our King and captain, crucified Saviour, alive in glory He now stands. Receive all the glory, our strength, honour and love, from now until we breathe our last. Amen.*

4. Fight the good fight

'This charge I entrust to you, Timothy, my child, in accordance with the prophecies previously made about you, that by them you may wage the good warfare'
(1 Tim. 1:18, ESV)

At CVM we take on a 'grand challenge' each year. It's simple really: do something to raise a thousand pounds or more for CVM. I chose to compete in a triathlon called The Gauntlet. This is essentially half the size of an Ironman Triathlon but made up of the same components. A mile of open water swimming, a 56-mile bike race, then a half marathon run. As soon as I signed up for it I knew it was a mistake.

The training was gruelling, and to be honest beat me on more than one occasion. I struggled with the running. Mile after mile I would battle the voices in my head saying, 'Give up! It's hurting – stop! Round the next corner have a sit down and some food.'

Paul is writing to Timothy here, training him to be a gospel man and 'charging' him to wage the good warfare. To stand firm, not be shaken or pushed from side to side, keeping the main thing, the main thing!

See, around Timothy at that point were a load of people turning away from the gospel, looking to anything but the work of Jesus on the cross, and ultimately being spiritually shipwrecked. Paul is urging Timothy, with great force and determination, to keep going and keep fighting; to keep Jesus and His cross in his focus and spend himself on that goal.

What does that have to do with you? What's the key here? Well, Timothy was equipped for the job. He knew it and so did Paul – and I believe we are equipped too!

Paul talks about some prophecies that had been spoken over Timothy that had confirmed the gift or gifts that God had given him for this spiritual punch-up (1 Tim. 4:14). Timothy's gifts seem to have been around leadership and being able to share the good news in a way that people understood, and he was being told to use them!

To stand firm, not be shaken or pushed from side to side

So here is the point: there is a spiritual punch-up going on for our families, our communities, our mates and even our churches. This book is to remind us that this fight is a spiritual one, and we need gospel men to emerge and advance. We are not the answer but the vessel, we are not the force but a broken army rebuilt, and we are the sons gifted for the Father's work.

Part of this call to forge gospel men reveals a deep call to pray and discover how God has equipped you for this rumble. So how about it? What has God armed you with to make a stand against the armies of hell and see lives of men saved around you?

As I wrote that line, I had a few pictures, and they went like this: 'Oh, the alarm has gone off early so I can pray and meet Jesus, but I'm tired today; maybe tomorrow.' 'I'm so busy at the moment, I just can't find the time to pray and read my Bible.' 'Once I have finished these other priorities I will set time aside to pray.' Men, there will be a host of things that come to your mind when the Holy Spirit starts to call you out to meet Him and do some business in prayer.

I charge you: stand and fight, make the time, carve it into your day so that nothing dare take its place. Believe that God wants to use you as a gospel man to cut through the armies of hell and rush a few machine gun nests. Believe you are equipped for this highest calling and get ready to see God do the impossible around you. Or you can always roll over in bed again and hit snooze. Your call.

Prayer-action

Pray this prayer and let it take root in your life: *Jesus, help us to know how we are equipped for this fight. Inspire us, Jesus, to stand and fight, to be men of prayer and focused on the Bible. Remind us of the men who have gone before us in Your name, and forge us, Lord, into gospel men, keeping You front and centre in all we do. Amen.*

we are the sons
gifted for the
Father's work

5. Salvation

'I urge, then, first of all, that petitions, prayers, intercession and thanksgiving be made for all people – for kings and all those in authority, that we may live peaceful and quiet lives in all godliness and holiness. This is good, and pleases God our Saviour, who wants all people to be saved and to come to a knowledge of the truth. For there is one God and one mediator between God and mankind, the man Christ Jesus, who gave himself as a ransom for all people. This has now been witnessed to at the proper time.' (1 Tim. 2:1-6)

I love films, and action films in particular. I am not a big superhero movie fan; I prefer action films like *Commando* and *Predator*. However, I do remember watching *Superman*

Returns (2006) and enjoying one particularly great moment in the film. Superman takes Lois up into the atmosphere, to about 30,000 feet. A couple of immediate issues arise: why is she not cold, and how is she breathing so effortlessly? Well, obviously, Superman radiates nuclear warmth if he needs to and he also breathes out oxygen not carbon dioxide, so she was buddy breathing. Anyway…

As they are in this moment, Lois is probably wondering if Superman will leave his life as a superhero and help her finish her loft extension, but Superman asks Lois what she can hear. She replies with, 'Nothing.' He then says something like, 'You wrote in your paper that the world doesn't need a saviour, but I hear them calling for one all the time.'

The world needs a saviour but we so often look out and fail to see it. We see people, mates, colleagues, family members, who look like they have everything sorted: car, home, family, jobs, food in the cupboard and bills getting paid. But the Bible says that when Jesus looked out at people, He saw through all this 'stuff' to a spiritual desperation.

'When he saw the crowds, he had compassion on them, because they were harassed and helpless, like sheep without a shepherd' (Matt. 9:36).

In this section from Paul's letter, Paul is telling Timothy to 'intercede'. One definition describes intercession as to 'fall in with someone'. Basically it's about holding someone up in prayer and hanging on; going for it to see stuff change and things happen. In this case, Paul is urging Timothy to really

The world needs a saviour

carry this load of people and their need to know salvation in their hearts. To see through the veneer around him and grasp the deep need in people's lives to hear about and know Jesus and the life He has for them.

In just three verses, Paul's letter effectively pulls the pin on a gospel grenade and rolls it to Timothy:

1.   God loves all men. He is a saviour and wants to lose no one (v4).
2.   We've got only one God and one mediator; a perfect God-man who stands in the gap between God and man. Jesus is His name (v5).
3.   This Jesus gave Himself as a ransom; a debt was owed for your freedom, and this man paid it – you can be free (v6).

As you think about sharpening your faith and the importance of mentoring others and being mentored, get to grips with the key of salvation. I love talking about salvation with people. I say to them, 'Tell me how you found Jesus – what's the story? How did it happen?' Talk together about what Jesus has done, and read over the Gospel accounts of His resurrection, listen to preachers declare the work of salvation, 'fall in' with someone to see a renewed love for the work of salvation. Why? Because this will plunge you into something of the mystery of what Jesus is all about, and it will awaken a heart to see the lost and the broken set free.

Prayer-action

Make this prayer your own: *Jesus, take us into the wonder of salvation, the mystery of Your great love for us, that we can be saved. Put a fire in our bellies for salvation and grant us the sight to see through the veneer to a hurting world in need of truth and life. One God, one mediator, sharpen salvation's edge in our lives, Jesus. Amen.*

Talk together about what Jesus has done

6.   The *S* word

'For Adam was formed first, then
Eve. And Adam was not the one
deceived; it was the woman who
was deceived and became a
sinner.' (1 Tim. 2:13-14)

I remember one time when I was playing a PlayStation game
online with a load of guys from all over the world. We were
in this one particular chat room, getting ready to storm a
legion of alien invaders and rescue precious resources from
them, and the guys started talking about Jesus.

As a Christian I should have been in there, but I was
nervous and held back. This one bloke, a Canadian guy, was
going for it. Not in a weird kind of way that switches people
off, but just being honest about his faith; no shame or fear.

He even said the '*S* word'! Yep, he told these guys that
the Bible calls our rebellion towards God 'sin', which has
happened and has infected us all like an internet virus.
I remember literally holding my breath, almost wanting to

a real condition in our lives today

pretend that my internet connection had gone down and leave the lobby.

Why? Well, the truth is that I was embarrassed to tell people that I believe sin is a real condition in our lives today and there is only one place to get it removed.

Now this section in the Bible can be a bit of puzzle to read, especially without any reflection on the situation and context in which Paul was writing this stuff. The Church then was in a bad way: men were looking to mixed gospel teaching and women were causing huge division outside and inside the Church.

Paul talks about Eve being deceived by the devil and deciding to eat the fruit from the tree of life. Adam was with her and he too ate the fruit. The Bible records that Eve had the conversation, a direct influence and disobedience, and Adam followed. Here's the deal – the outcome is: both sinned.

This moment in history was like a slip on two gigantic tectonic plates. 'Doubt' smashed into 'lie' and a tsunami was triggered, the wave impacting any human, no matter who they are, where or when they are born, what they look like or what language they speak.

The 'doubt' – 'Did God really say this?' The 'lie' – 'You won't die!'

The *S* word was born: *sin*.

What's the point of all this? Well, part of our being forged into gospel men means that we know what this is about and we unashamedly stand on the truth of the Bible that says, 'all have sinned and fall short of the glory of God' (Rom. 3:23).

I learnt a lot from that Canadian fella. I have tried to dress up the gospel so it looks 'better', more palatable, easier on the eye and ear. But this is something we can take great confidence in: sin is disastrous news for the world, but the blood of Jesus that was shed at the cross is the best news ever! As you mentor and build gospel men, and as you yourself are built in the fullness of who God is calling you to be, know this – Jesus called out on the cross, and this is what He said: 'It is finished.' Have some of that!

 Prayer-action

Pray this prayer and think about what it means for you: *Jesus, help us to fearlessly announce the good news of Your cross, but may we never hide the reason for it. Help us communicate sin to our world in a way that removes nothing of its reality, but includes everything of Your victory. Amen.*

7. Who are you on a Monday?

'He must also have a good reputation with outsiders, so that he will not fall into disgrace and into the devil's trap.' (1 Tim. 3:7)

In this next section of his letter, Paul is guiding Timothy about how he can help men be equipped and developed into the right kind of men for serving the Church. Paul sets out some spiritual conditions, if you like, for these men and the leaders of the Church. This is important, of course, but then Paul drops in a really interesting bit about actually living a good example or 'testimony' outside the church environment.

Christian author Bill Hybels wrote a book called, *Who You Are When No One's Looking*. That got me thinking about another way of saying this: 'Who are you on a Monday?'

I'm not saying that my title is better, of course, but what I have discovered is that it is really easy for Christian men to disappear into the 'professional' Christian routines on a

Sunday and then almost leave their faith on the shelf until the following week.

I remember asking a bloke recently what he does on a Sunday. He replied, 'Oh, my job is to unpack the church from the cupboard on a Sunday, then after the service I pack it all away again.' He was talking about the sound system equipment, the chairs, the box with the custard creams in, and all the other 'stuff' that usually accompanies a 'regular' church service. I asked him if he meant he 'unpacks the church' practically or spiritually. I got a blank response.

I used to live my Christian life like that. Sunday would come around and off we'd go to church because that's what we do, and I learnt the acceptable behaviour for that routine. Guess what? That's the sort of lukewarm worship God spits out. Neither hot nor cold, just tepid!

Does that sound a bit harsh? Well, fellas, let's get real. Men all around us – our mates, brothers, fathers, sons and uncles – are heading down a dangerous path that leads nowhere good, and we can so easily settle for a lukewarm Sunday that fails to impact our heads and hearts during the week.

Being gospel men means we need to have a blameless walk outside the church community on a Sunday. We should walk unashamed, feet on the narrow path, hearts and heads set on the prize, fighting to stay there. Who we are on a Sunday is who we are at home with our children and wives. Who we are on a Sunday is who we are at school, at college, at university, in the boardroom, in the pub, at the gym, on the football terraces.

As you refine this faith and become gospel men, this is where the rubber hits the road; this is the arena where battle will commence. When you set foot into your week on a Monday, the fight for consistency, integrity, honour, courage and holiness will begin.

What's the secret? I think it is in preparation. Prayer, committed study of the Bible, accountability, accessibility to one another when the fire is hot, honesty and undefended hearts. Get that going and you will see giant leaps forward as gospel men with a blameless testimony outside of 'church life'.

 Prayer-action

Pray this in your own words, or use the words here: *Jesus, help us to be men of integrity, blameless in all we do. May we keep our hearts soft to Your call and Your Word. Help us, Jesus, to be men who follow You full time, in every compartment of our hearts and lives. Amen.*

8. Be on your guard, son

'Now the Spirit expressly says
that in later times some will
depart from the faith by devoting
themselves to deceitful spirits
and teachings of demons'
(1 Tim. 4:1, ESV)

My grandfather Bill was a rifleman during the Second World War. He survived, but not without his scars. My dad recalls a story that my grandfather only ever told once, and was never spoken about again after that. My grandfather spoke of a moment before his hospitalisation in Italy when he and his close friend walked behind the tracks of an allied tank. The order had been to stay with both feet inside the tracks made by the tank's treads, and not to deviate from that path. On this occasion, my grandfather's friend, needing the toilet, walked just metres towards a hedge on his left and stepped on a mine. The triggered explosion killed my grandad's friend instantly, hospitalised my grandfather and took away his hearing.

As we train and sharpen ourselves as gospel men, it is essential that we stay on the narrow path, keeping our feet on the one true rock and source of life. It is so easy to be enchanted by impressive graphics, presentations and slick strategies that will 'change your life'. But the real power, this saving grace, was messy! A man was flogged, beaten, spat on and falsely accused. He was dressed as a mock king and punched and insulted. His clothes were gambled away and a crown of thorns was pushed onto His head to add insult to His final moments. This man was stretched out in agony by others and nailed to a cross, lifted up for all to see and marvel at His shame.

On that cross the author of life was made sin. All the world's mess and failure, disobedience and shame, was lumped with Him. He called out that 'it is finished' and gave up His life. Silence, confusion and fear swept over the friends of Jesus as they gathered and slowly began to unfold the events of the last few years. Then, early on the third day, the greatest miracle to have ever touched the earth began: the tomb stone was rolled away and life was returned.

Jesus appeared to hundreds of people over a period of weeks. He ate with them, walked with them and declared to them that death had been overcome! The doubters were not pushed away but brought closer to really see. The fearful and shameful were reinstated and put back on their feet. A promise of life to come and a message was born. Salvation – death had been defeated and sin had lost its sting.

In Jesus, we can repent of our sins, and we can believe the greatest miracle of all and find life. Paul is instructing Timothy to be a good worker in the gospel. Men and even a church had begun to 'depart' and move away from this true gospel about Jesus. Our challenge today as gospel men is to never let our feet wander from that path. Stay the course and keep your eyes fixed on Jesus, the author and perfecter of your faith.

 # Prayer-action

Pray this and remember that you should be prepared to respond when God answers the prayer: *Jesus, help us to never lose sight of You and the cross. Help us to be men who unashamedly announce the message of salvation. Train our hands and our minds to work for us, as gospel men, on the right path and determined to keep our feet in place, following You. Amen.*

9. Physical and spiritual workouts

'If you put these things before the brothers, you will be a good servant of Christ Jesus, being trained in the words of the faith and of the good doctrine that you have followed. Have nothing to do with irreverent, silly myths. Rather train yourself for godliness; for while bodily training is of some value, godliness is of value in every way, as it holds promise for the present life and also for the life to come.' (1 Tim. 4:6-8, ESV)

Let's carry on from the last chapter, as Paul is constantly encouraging Timothy to be a gospel man. Recently I was chatting to two fellas on the same day. The first bloke was a pro bodybuilder – he was massive. As we were talking, I could see other blokes looking at him from the corner of

You will have to feed on the truth

their eyes. This guy was up at 4.30am each day to train and you could tell – he had arms like sculpted lumps of bronze. To achieve those results would have taken commitment, discipline and continual nourishment on the right stuff.

The second man I spoke to that day was in his late sixties – a small, grey-haired and gentle-spirited man. As we spoke, I asked him about his walk with God and if he had anything he could share. What unfolded in the next few minutes was like the physical strength of the first man but without the honed delts, traps and pectorals; this older man was a *spiritual* heavyweight who knew the Word of God.

He immediately opened a Bible he had on him, and set about sharing a few moments in his life using God's Word, the Bible, to signpost these various times. He shared the wins and fails, the cost and the call he had lived through, and it was incredible. This man had trained his hand with the Bible – he knew where to go in God's Word and he knew the work of the Holy Spirit to help him understand it.

Here's the thing, fellas: as you aspire to be a gospel man and train or be trained as such, it will require effort. You will have to feed on the truth, training and building yourself up to know God's Word and letting it shape your life.

In today's passage, Paul is talking about this from the perspective of an athlete training and making a commitment. I like that. How you go about doing this, and where and when, is going to vary from guy to guy. The point is that we are men who know God's Word and we have trained our hands for the spiritual war. Within us are the spiritual 'muscles' my pro bodybuilder has got, and we have the potential to get into tip-top shape and condition. Sinful men, saved by grace, now sons and brothers trained for war.

Speak God's Word out, text it to men around you, say it out over the phone, email it, print it and learn it. Gospel men are honed and nourished by the Word of God.

 Prayer-action

Open your Bible and read it. Invite God to be working through what you read to change your life and the lives of the men around you.

10. Don't fear the man!

'Don't let anyone look down on you because you are young, but set an example for the believers in speech, in conduct, in love, in faith and in purity.' (1 Tim. 4:12)

Personally, I believe that one of the things we can intentionally build into a generation of men being shaped for evangelism is to live beyond fear. Younger men need older men to speak into their lives, to guide them, to encourage them and sharpen their vision.

Fear is perhaps one of our enemy's most efficient weapons to numb and blunt any mighty courage and risk-taking for the gospel. The 'what ifs' and the moments of 'suppose'.

'What would the lads think if they knew I went to church?' 'Where can I hide my Bible or my face, when the conversation starts going into why religion is so destructive?' 'Suppose I start to share Jesus then get a tough question I can't answer, then what?'

I was in Serbia a while ago and spent some time chatting to a few of the guys there after a meeting. One particular guy was talking with me about fear and how we can fear the man, whatever shape or form that represents: men of influence over us or the fear of ridicule or even persecution for sticking our necks out and sharing the truth about Jesus.

This guy said to me, 'Maybe, Nathan, the answer then is perfect love, because that is capable of driving out all fear.' As we love those who ridicule, challenge, disagree or even hate us, something profound will happen.

Let's put this another way: '"Love the Lord your God with all your heart and with all your soul and with all your strength and with all your mind"; and, "Love your neighbour as yourself"' (Luke 10:27).

When we do that we find a way to live beyond fear. Fearful situations and moments are part of our human life, but the way to live beyond these is to put our love in the right place. Love God, and then love others. From that place our conduct – our lives – will be stuffed full of love and we won't be able to hide it.

I think that, as we forge gospel men who can live beyond fear, we need to invest in what it means to really love people. To choose to bless when we are being cursed, and to choose to love when we are being hated, is incredible and is not something you will find in a book entitled 'How to Overcome Your Biggest Fears'. This can only be discovered in a relationship with Jesus, daily looking to Him for your strength and guidance.

Here is the most amazing thing: I think that as Jesus looked out, even at the men with the hammers driving the nails into His hands and feet, He loved them. What He did on the cross was for those boys too. The bloke who told barefaced lies about Jesus in court – Jesus loved him. The person who wove the crown of thorns and the solider who pushed it onto Jesus' head were loved by Jesus too. You and me, with all our baggage and empty promises, our 'in and out' commitment to the name of Jesus and His mission… He loves us too.

Amazing.

 Prayer-action

Make this your own prayer:
Jesus, help us to invest in the men around us to be gospel men. Help us to love the lost and live beyond fear as we advance with the good news. Shape us and equip us with boldness and courage to unashamedly build Your kingdom. Amen.

11. Devote yourself

'Meditate on these things; give yourself entirely to them, that your progress may be evident to all.' (1 Tim. 4:15, NKJV)

The language here is really challenging as Paul urges Timothy on in the gospel, telling him, 'give yourself entirely to them'. That makes me a bit nervous, if I am honest. How about you?

This book is in part about what you need to give as, or receive from, a mentor to be a gospel man, but there is also a part here for you, and to be honest the biggest action is yours. Devote yourself to this – to the gospel – the Word and work of Jesus Christ. Make Him everything. Be consumed by Him, invest in the relationship and make Him your treasure.

At the time of writing this, my son is six years old, and he is devoted to the game *Minecraft*.

He wakes me up talking about it; he makes me ask him

How devoted are we to Jesus and the gospel?

questions about it when I put him to bed. He has set up a *Minecraft* corner where we game together. He has drawn posters and designed logos and banners for the area. We have a YouTube channel where we post gameplay we record together as we play the game. He is, as I've said, devoted to it. I even made him a *Minecraft* cake for his sixth birthday – it was amazing!

How devoted are we to Jesus and the gospel? Are we as devoted as my son is to *Minecraft*? Does it give us our purpose and something to aim for when we get up in the morning? Does it fill our every waking moment? When we go to bed do we start to imagine what tomorrow will bring – ready for another day spent absolutely devoted to our cause?

The idea of forging gospel men through intentional and focused mentoring is great, but it is pointless if you only pray and read the Bible when you have a mentoring session coming up. Our ultimate mentor and guide, our master and commander, King and brother is Jesus, and He wants to speak with you each day.

When Paul tasks Timothy to advance, to progress, he

uses a military term that has force behind it. The point is that Timothy was already charging forward. He was having an impact around him for God's kingdom – he had serious momentum.

I remember being in Brazil and living in a rehabilitation centre with my family. Talk about a trial by fire! One night a couple of the lads knocked on my door and invited me over to the main meeting room. When I got there, 30 blokes were showered, hair slicked back, sitting in clean shirts and trousers with their Bibles on their laps. 'Can you share something with us, please, Nathan? Tell us about Jesus and what God is like.'

The complete panic in my head must have been evident to the guys but I held my nerve. This sort of thing needed to be planned for! I had no PowerPoint or clever slides or stories to use. They looked at me, just expecting me to be seeking God each day, and therefore I must have something to share with them. A man of God, devoted to the Master's mission, would be equipped and ready on all occasions! I wasn't... that day!

Devotion like this can come through necessity or discipline, but I believe it is focused around intimacy and revelation. Jesus wants us to know Him, really know Him and have an incredible, intimate relationship with Him. In that framework, revelation happens; God's Word reveals truth to us, in us and through us. The purpose is to build the kingdom and call sons home. To see lives and families, communities and societies, impacted by the life, death and resurrection of Jesus.

I am devoted to Jesus, His mission and this relationship. How about you?

Prayer-action

Spend some time today with Jesus; your relationship with Him is key. What does devotion to Jesus and His mission look like for you? It could impact your time, your wallet, your hopes, your dreams and even how and what you pray…

12. Honour, even when that bloke's got it wrong

'Do not rebuke an older man, but exhort *him* as a father, younger men as brothers, older women as mothers, younger women as sisters, with all purity.'
(1 Tim. 5:1-2, NKJV)

Respect and honour, even when someone has got it wrong, don't mean we have to ignore wrongdoing or just pretend it's not happening and will go away. We need to deal with stuff in the right way. Gospel men need to be steered and guided by others; that's what iron sharpening iron does (see Prov. 27:17).

I remember being taken to a war museum by our hosts in the country we were travelling in. The museum had some huge cannons outside that would have been set up behind the artillery to aim the shell and deliver it on target. One of the guys I was with, Suneel, heads up CVM's international work.

Suneel stood behind the gun and said something like, 'Let's land something significant this year with CVM, on target!'

That got me thinking. We have guys up and down the UK visiting churches, men's groups, eating breakfasts, and telling men about Jesus. We have wild evangelists who are sold out for Jesus and on His mission. The thing is, every now and then I need to adjust the direction wheel on the artillery gun. Just a few clicks to the left or to the right can ensure we land our vision on target.

But sometimes it's not easy to turn the wheel. Sometimes it means a difficult email or conversation, which might get misunderstood and then require five other emails or phone calls to sort out. But that's OK – it's what has to happen sometimes.

Part of this mentoring gospel men thing is dealing with stuff with respect and honour. Not being afraid to call things out when they stink. In the verses we read today, Paul is urging Timothy to deal with things in the right way,

Gospel men need to be steered and guided by others

with honour and respect, to confront things and build them up stronger than they were before.

This is so important in our intentional relationships of building gospel men. As we go into these relationships we can do it with an undefended heart. This means that we can take the instruction and correction, and we can give it out too in the right way. It's not easy on both counts but essential in building us up stronger for the fight. We will have stuff to deal with in our lives – it might be laying low, hoping not to be seen, or it might be glaringly obvious. The point is that we need to be ready to deal with it in the right ways.

 ## **Prayer-action**

Ask God today to help you keep your heart right, and to speak with honour and respect when dealing with the difficult stuff. Be ready to stand together with your brothers when things are not how they should be, and fight together to be sharp, gospel men.

13. Keep your heart right with money

'Now godliness with contentment is great gain. For we brought nothing into *this* world, *and it is* certain we can carry nothing out. And having food and clothing, with these we shall be content. But those who desire to be rich fall into temptation and a snare, and *into* many foolish and harmful lusts which drown men in destruction and perdition. For the love of money is a root of all *kinds of* evil, for which some have strayed from the faith in their greediness, and pierced themselves through with many sorrows.' (1 Tim. 6:6-10, NKJV)

a continual focus on listening to God

Paul is still teaching Timothy here in the context of false teachers and how easily they can be taken from the right path. The interesting thing is that this can be true of anyone who is seeking to live a holy life.

On a recent trip to Brazil I was amazed at seeing one Christian man's heart towards money. This guy is a Brazilian and earns about £200 a month. He had recently received a gift of about £800 and I was astonished at what he decided to do with it.

His first thought – not his second or twenty-fifth – his *first* thought was, 'How can I invest this in God's work?' Now I am not saying you must do this; the point is that he has a continual focus on listening to God and being ready to act even when it means paying the bill!

He spent the lot – he hired an amazing retreat venue for two days, paid for it and invited 60 families. He bought all the food, all the drink and cake. He even drove around picking anyone up who couldn't get there. He then spent his time cleaning, helping to cook and ensuring that everything went well. He paid for a few speakers to come and bring some teaching from the Bible, and he did all that from the side-line. No one except me and a few others knew that he had paid for it all; a man with literally just enough per month to feed his family and pay his bills.

I asked him about it afterwards, and why he did it. He simply told me, 'Nathan, I just wanted people to have an opportunity to meet Jesus as a family.'

The process of being forged into gospel men will mean that at some points on that journey it can hurt. This guy could have spent that dosh on himself and his family, and no one would have thought anything of it as that would have been fine. But he was convinced that it could do even more, and it did! We launched CVM Brazil at that event, and it has continued to grow.

You haven't got to run out and sell everything you have to run a similar event, that's not the point. The point is keeping our hearts right and open enough so that when God puts His hand on our wallet, we respond. We manage to hold these things – money, possessions, even time – lightly, and perhaps look for ways to be radical gospel men of generosity.

at some points
on that journey
it can hurt

Prayer-action

Say these words to God (and mean them!), or use your own words:

Jesus, help us to keep our hearts right, and help us to never preach and teach anything other than the truth of the cross. Help us to be ready and listening to Your voice, even if that means settling a bill or two. Broaden our generosity, then let us see the glory You receive. Amen.

14. Be encouraged, man of God!

'But you, O man of God, flee these things and pursue righteousness, godliness, faith, love, patience, gentleness. Fight the good fight of faith, lay hold on eternal life, to which you were also called and have confessed the good confession in the presence of many witnesses.'
(1 Tim. 6:11-12, NKJV)

My brother Ben ran the London Marathon a few years ago. The event is made up of various sponsors and you can run for a charity or group. Each runner, including my bro, had their name and number pinned onto their t-shirt.

As he came running through, you could hear random people shouting his name and cheering him on, just getting behind him and encouraging him and all the other runners by name. It was a great feeling for that brief moment;

a genuine cheer of encouragement.

In today's reading Paul is still encouraging Timothy, and on the back of the money talk we looked at in the previous chapter, he is urging Timothy on to keep the faith and pursue godliness in his life. What stands out for me is that Paul opens with the line 'man of God'!

If you have read the New Testament before, you will have seen how much Paul was used by God in the most amazing ways to get the truth out and the gospel heard. Incredible stuff. If Paul were writing to me and started with the words 'man of God', I would put that in a frame and it would encourage me for a long time.

Yes, Paul was an influential man for the kingdom and God used his life – weakness and all – to build the Church, but it is bigger than that. Paul had poured his life into Timothy's; he had been investing in this young man so he would be a 'man of God'.

Not only is that encouraging for Timothy, it is a call for us to do the same. Who are you investing in this week, building up and encouraging to be the next man of God? Who is he? Where is he? Is he on your mind and heart? Do you commit yourself to encourage, build up and pray for that bloke? Is that happening for you?

It is suggested that Paul wrote this just after his first release from Roman prison, and the next letter to Timothy while in prison in Rome again, shortly before his death.

Why is that important? Well, these letters, which we

now know as 1 Timothy and 2 Timothy, deal with so much: the Church, ensuring the right teaching is happening and leaders are being put into place, keeping sound doctrine and more. But for me, within these letters is a continual investment in Timothy, building him up, intentionally encouraging him and 'charging' him to be the gospel man Paul had inspired him to be.

As we invest in others or are being invested in, to be leaders, gospel men and culture shifters, let's encourage each other, call out the pitfalls and celebrate the wins. Let's build the men of God, invest in them and, like Paul, be part of Jesus' kingdom builders.

 ## Prayer-action

Pray something along these lines, and then be ready for when God answers that prayer: *Jesus, help us to encourage and be encouraged as men of God. Build our faith and hope in You that we may boldly stand in our time and generation to point to You. All the glory be Yours, our God and our King. Amen.*

15. Guard it, son, and it will grow!

'Timothy, guard what has been entrusted to your care.'
(1 Tim. 6:20)

OK, bear with me here... remember the verse from Philippians 2:22 that we opened this book with: 'as a son with his father he [Timothy] has served with me in the work of the gospel'?

When my first child was born I felt an overwhelming weight of responsibility; that something had been entrusted to me, something money couldn't buy and was too precious even to have monetary value. This child was like a deposit into my life and my care, something to guard and treasure. Something that would captivate my waking hours; an investment and something that would grow.

This verse from Paul is like a call to the deep – the passing on of something so special, so precious, that no value can ever be assigned to it. The actual Hebrew word used in the phrase 'entrusted to your care' means 'deposit' – a deposit

We have been given the most amazing news

that has been entrusted into the hands of Timothy, for him to guard and nurture.

This is such an important and central key in forging gospel men. We have been given the most amazing news: the mystery of salvation and eternity has been unveiled and shown to us in the person of Jesus. We have the good news, the hope of the nations and a message that can impact the blokes around us for the rest of their lives on earth and into eternity, 10,000 years from now and on and on and on forever.

This process of intentionally building gospel men – men confident in the Word of God and men who know and love their saviour – will change everything. I like to imagine Paul penning this letter to Timothy with a sense of satisfaction in the man Timothy was becoming. Paul had been able to live his life sold out for Jesus, impact the eternity of countless people and shake the gates of hell. He went on a mad mission with Jesus, rescuing men from the path to hell and setting them on the narrow path for eternity. Amazing. But he was also able to instil it, nurture it and grow it in the heart of Timothy – 'as a son with his father he [Timothy] has served with me in the work of the gospel'.

The heart of this book is about multiplication. This investment, this guarding the true message – the gospel – will multiply and bring fruit and life. Paul knew it and poured out his life into Timothy so he would then do the same.

What about you? Are you up for this? Are you ready for what this can be?

The next section of this book is designed to give you some material to intentionally begin to build this in. Based on what we have already explored, it is time to invest in making gospel men.

 Prayer-action

Spend some time asking God who you need to invest in or who you need to approach to ask to invest in your life. Pray that God will open up a way for this to begin, and set a fire in your heart for the work of making gospel men.

Part 3

Explore, identify and commit

Recently at The Gathering, CVM's annual men's festival, I was sitting with a fantastic guy called Raul. Raul is part of the team of men who are led by Graham Kendrick at The Gathering, leading sung worship.

When I went into the worship tent, Raul was sitting there, working on some music and eating a Pot Noodle. I asked him a few questions about God and the Bible and he pulled a Gideon's Bible from his bag and started to tell me about keys in the Bible to pass faith on. Awesome – he didn't know I was writing this book about keys for building gospel men.

When I left Raul I walked through the mud to the mess tent where we were showing Wales play in the Euros. I sat with a load of guys from the church I used to serve as pastor and got chatting with one called Paul, in his twenties, and I started to share with him in the same way Raul had done with me. Paul asked, 'Mate, how have you got all this stuff in your head, ready to go?' I said to him, 'Mate,' (lots of 'mates' in Essex) 'I have literally just walked out of that tent into this one, and a guy has just given this stuff to me, and I am passing it on to you!'

It was a very cool moment – this is how it should work! We sit under the wisdom and direction of other godly men, then we pass it on to men looking to us. This isn't to say we don't need Jesus as our guide and the Holy Spirit to intercede and move in our hearts and minds. The role of mentoring like this is to sharpen, to forge and build, to call out and walk the narrow path together – always looking to Jesus and being equipped by the Holy Spirit.

With that said, let's drill into some of these studies for you to do with a mate.

This is not a prescriptive course in biblical studies; it is simply designed to get you talking, focused and with your Bible open.

The studies

So here are four studies that will get you into the Bible. It's good to pray about the study before you meet up and again when you're together. Invite the Holy Spirit to bring direction and to inspire and shape the time you'll have together with God and with your mate.

Before you meet up, you might like to start by reading the background information and the verses in order to get an overview of the Bible passages you'll be looking at. You can always refer to the background information when you're together, but it's good to get yourself grounded in it a bit before getting going with someone else.

Then it's time to get out your Bibles (or Bible apps) and start reading. Read the passages of the Bible slowly and try not to rush through them. Allow the meaning of each word and sentence to sink in before reading on. This might mean it takes a while, but go slowly – it's life-changing stuff so it's worth a bit more time and effort. It might even help to read it through a couple of times, maybe in different Bible translations, to see what jumps out at you.

Once you've read it through, you might want to just have a think together about your initial ideas and reactions. You can then delve into the questions, which have been split into 'Explore', 'Identify' and 'Commit' sections to help you break them down and apply what you're learning to your life, not just gain head-knowledge.

Don't try to do every single question in a schoolroom kind of way where you ask and they answer, one question after the other without much processing. Do the questions that will help you and your mate really get to grips with it and bring about life-change. Try to get to the core point that the question is aiming to get at – mull it over and chat it over. Come up with your own questions as well, tailored to the specific theme or Bible passage – bringing out the things you want to get to grips with as you go through it with your mate.

Don't be afraid if the conversation goes off-piste a bit, so long as you don't end up talking about cars for an hour! You're there to learn more about God in order to bring about life-change in both of you – you'll hopefully find that you learn just as much as the guy you're meeting with. So if you end up looking at a different part of the Bible from the one you intended to look at, or discussing some other aspect of God or His kingdom than what you were 'supposed' to be discussing – don't worry!

Remember that 'All Scripture is God-breathed and is useful for teaching, rebuking, correcting and training in righteousness' (1 Tim. 3:16) – it's all good! It could be that God is directing you towards another topic or verse He wants you to learn from. You might end up going from one thing to another, but as long as God and the gospel are right at the core of the conversation, there shouldn't be anything to worry about.

That said, try not to go on a wild goose chase – be alert to which topics of conversation are genuine and which ones are just an excuse to not talk about the real issue at hand. The more you meet with your mate and get to know him, the better sense of direction you'll have in the conversation.

Have a bit of back-and-forth and some banter. Don't make it a dull learning exercise – bring it to life and make it a free-flowing discussion. The passion you put into it will show that this stuff really means something to you – that the Bible isn't just words on the page but is the living Word of God: powerful, authoritative, always showing new things no matter how many times you read the same part, always shining light into the darkness in new ways.

End with prayer. Invite the Holy Spirit to fuse all this into your heart and mind, and build it into your life each day. Pray boldly, take ground and expect the impossible!

And there you have it – you've done a Bible study without it feeling like a 'study' at all!

 **Bible Study 1:**

The cross

Bible book

1 Corinthians

Date

Around AD 55

Author and target audience

The apostle Paul, writing to a church in Corinth that he had
founded on a missionary journey there (Acts 18:1). Paul was
helped by two Jewish believers, Priscilla and Aquila. He was
also joined by Silas and Timothy, and preached in the
synagogues there. The city had a lot going on, including
about a thousand 'religious' prostitutes for the Greek
goddess of love, Aphrodite. A challenging culture in which
to share the cross of Jesus!

Themes

Part of the purpose of Paul's letter to the church here is to
outline the right teaching and structure for this new
collection of Christians. He dealt with issues of disunity, sin
in the church, marriage, worship, roles of men and women,
spiritual gifts and more.

Verses

1 Corinthians 2:1-5

'And so it was with me, brothers and sisters. When I came to you, I did not come with eloquence or human wisdom as I proclaimed to you the testimony about God. For I resolved to know nothing while I was with you except Jesus Christ and him crucified. I came to you in weakness with great fear and trembling. My message and my preaching were not with wise and persuasive words, but with a demonstration of the Spirit's power, so that your faith might not rest on human wisdom, but on God's power.'

Bible book

Isaiah

Date

739-686 BC

Author and target audience

Isaiah was a prophet in Judah during the reign of four kings of Judah. A married man with two sons, he was used by God to speak out to the people. Even though Isaiah knew that his calling out and speaking prophecy to the people would largely be in vain, he stepped forward as God's man, a choice that ultimately ended horribly for him when he was sawn in two with a wooden saw (according to some historical texts).

Themes

Isaiah was speaking to people during a time of division between two kingdoms, but his main focus was on the southern kingdom, Judah. His voice called out under the direction of God into many different situations: political, spiritual and relational. He spoke with authority into the moment he was in, the days that were to come soon, and even the five hundred plus years beyond, to Jesus the Christ.

Verses

Isaiah 53

'Who has believed our message
and to whom has the arm of the LORD been revealed?
He grew up before him like a tender shoot,
and like a root out of dry ground.
He had no beauty or majesty to attract us to him,
nothing in his appearance that we should desire him.
He was despised and rejected by mankind,
a man of suffering, and familiar with pain.
Like one from whom people hide their faces
he was despised, and we held him in low esteem.
Surely he took up our pain
and bore our suffering,
yet we considered him punished by God,
stricken by him, and afflicted.
But he was pierced for our transgressions,
he was crushed for our iniquities;

the punishment that brought us peace was on him,

and by his wounds we are healed.

We all, like sheep, have gone astray,

each of us has turned to our own way;

and the LORD has laid on him

the iniquity of us all.

He was oppressed and afflicted,

yet he did not open his mouth;

he was led like a lamb to the slaughter,

and as a sheep before its shearers is silent,

so he did not open his mouth.

By oppression and judgment he was taken away.

Yet who of his generation protested?

For he was cut off from the land of the living;

for the transgression of my people he was punished.

He was assigned a grave with the wicked,

and with the rich in his death,

though he had done no violence,

nor was any deceit in his mouth.

Yet it was the LORD's will to crush him and cause him to suffer,

and though the LORD makes his life an offering for sin,

he will see his offspring and prolong his days,

and the will of the LORD will prosper in his hand.

After he has suffered,

he will see the light of life and be satisfied;

by his knowledge my righteous servant will justify many,

and he will bear their iniquities.

Therefore I will give him a portion among the great,

and he will divide the spoils with the strong,

because he poured out his life unto death,

and was numbered with the transgressors.

For he bore the sin of many,

and made intercession for the transgressors.'

The Questions

Explore

What stood out for you when you were reading these Bible verses?

① *Paul highly educated, did not want to show off with his vocabulary. Stripped himself mentally, left it to God.*

Did any particular sentences or individual words hit you or raise some questions? If so, what were they?

② *The accuracy of Isaiah's prophecy.*

3 Did you get any answers?

_____

_____

4 ## Identify

What did you see in the verses that helped you see more of Jesus?

Stopping ourselves.??

_____

_____

5 What does the cross of Jesus mean to you?

If Jesus had not come, we would be in the dark, Jesus Gives us that love.

_____

6 What might the Holy Spirit be saying to you?

Was this question when we close.

_____

_____

Commit

(7) How can you see this applying to your life?

_____

_____

_____

(8) What can you put in place this week or month that will build on this revelation/discovery?

_____

_____

_____

(9) What do you need to be accountable for at the moment?

_____

_____

_____

(10) Don't let it drift to nothing – commit it to prayer and be accountable to update on it next session. You might like to write down some prayer and/or action points to remember.

– Sharing faith

Bible Study 2:
Repentance

Bible book
2 Peter

Date
Around AD 67-68

Author and target audience
The author of this letter is known as the apostle Peter. He was writing to a church at the time to offer some sound advice, even though he was in prison in Rome, facing death.

Themes
When Peter wrote this letter, the Church was infiltrated by loads of false teachers. He wrote to equip Christians to stand firm in their faith and in the true gospel that they had received. He also wrote the letter to help them to grow in their character and to be more like Jesus in all they did.

Verses
2 Peter 3:1-10
'Dear friends, this is now my second letter to you. I have written both of them as reminders to stimulate you to

wholesome thinking. I want you to recall the words spoken in the past by the holy prophets and the command given by our Lord and Saviour through your apostles.

Above all, you must understand that in the last days scoffers will come, scoffing and following their own evil desires. They will say, "Where is this 'coming' he promised? Ever since our ancestors died, everything goes on as it has since the beginning of creation." But they deliberately forget that long ago by God's word the heavens came into being and the earth was formed out of water and by water. By these waters also the world of that time was deluged and destroyed. By the same word the present heavens and earth are reserved for fire, being kept for the day of judgment and destruction of the ungodly.

But do not forget this one thing, dear friends: with the Lord a day is like a thousand years, and a thousand years are like a day. The Lord is not slow in keeping his promise, as some understand slowness. Instead he is patient with you, not wanting anyone to perish, but everyone to come to repentance.

But the day of the Lord will come like a thief. The heavens will disappear with a roar; the elements will be destroyed by fire, and the earth and everything done in it will be laid bare.'

Bible book

Psalms

Date

From about 1400 BC, for 900 years of Jewish history

Author and target audience

The book we know of as Psalms is perhaps best described as 'The Book of Praises', as it is a collection of praises in various forms and shapes by about seven different composers. However, King David, the same David who defeated Goliath, wrote 73 of the 150 psalms.

Themes

In the book of Psalms, or the Psalter as it can be called, you will find a collection of lived moments and shared experiences of calling out and focusing on God. These range from moments of epic wins and celebrations, individually and collectively, to epic fails, disasters and battles. All of these are reflections of lives lived in relationship with God and understood through His plans and promises.

Verses

Psalm 51:7-17

'Cleanse me with hyssop, and I shall be clean;
    wash me, and I shall be whiter than snow.

Let me hear joy and gladness;

    let the bones you have crushed rejoice.

Hide your face from my sins

    and blot out all my iniquity.

Create in me a pure heart, O God,

    and renew a steadfast spirit within me.

Do not cast me from your presence

    or take your Holy Spirit from me.

Restore to me the joy of your salvation

    and grant me a willing spirit, to sustain me.

Then I will teach transgressors your ways,

    so that sinners will turn back to you.

Deliver me from the guilt of bloodshed, O God,

    you who are God my Saviour,

    and my tongue will sing of your righteousness.

Open my lips, Lord,

    and my mouth will declare your praise.

You do not delight in sacrifice, or I would bring it;

    you do not take pleasure in burnt offerings.

My sacrifice, O God, is a broken spirit;

    a broken and contrite heart

    you, God, will not despise.'

The Questions

Explore *ok Pick 1 verse that stood out.*

What stood out for you when you were reading these
Bible verses?

_____

_____

_____

ok Did any part of it surprise you. Words/verses?

Did any particular sentences or individual words hit you or
raise some questions? If so, what were they?

_____

_____

_____

Did you get any answers?

_____

_____

_____

Some of the questions may seem personal/challenging. If so don't feel you have to share them.

Identify

What did you see in the verses that helped you see more of Jesus and better understand repentance?

Ps. Vs: 9. often the "stain", is impregnated in our mind - even though we are forgiven - the memory holds us back.

What does repentance mean to you? we sometime's can be quite participation stubborn

What might the Holy Spirit be saying about something specific in your life today?

Vs. 8. Dont be disheartened - because of the long wait.

Commit

How can you see this applying to your life?

As men do we Repent differently from Women?

What can you put in place this week or month that will
build on this revelation/discovery?

What do you need to be accountable for at the moment?

Don't let it drift to nothing - commit it to prayer and be
accountable to update on it next session. You might like to
write down some prayer and/or action points to remember.

Bible Study 3:
Forgiveness

Bible book

1 John

Date

About AD 90-95

Author and target audience

This letter doesn't state the author, but it is suggested that this is John, the apostle and disciple of Jesus. John lived in Ephesus when he was writing and was active in many churches, teaching, preaching and sharing the good news of Jesus, of which at this point he was probably the last remaining eye witness amongst all the disciples.

Themes

John's letter, like other letters, tackles the false teachers and ideas around salvation and forgiveness of sins. His letter is like a father instructing his children - pastoral, faith-building and reminding his readers of the character of Christians.

Verses

1 John 1:1-10

'That which was from the beginning, which we have heard, which we have seen with our eyes, which we have looked at and our hands have touched – this we proclaim concerning the Word of life. The life appeared; we have seen it and testify to it, and we proclaim to you the eternal life, which was with the Father and has appeared to us. We proclaim to you what we have seen and heard, so that you also may have fellowship with us. And our fellowship is with the Father and with his Son, Jesus Christ. We write this to make our joy complete.

This is the message we have heard from him and declare to you: God is light; in him there is no darkness at all. If we claim to have fellowship with him and yet walk in the darkness, we lie and do not live out the truth. But if we walk in the light, as he is in the light, we have fellowship with one another, and the blood of Jesus, his Son, purifies us from all sin.

If we claim to be without sin, we deceive ourselves and the truth is not in us. If we confess our sins, he is faithful and just and will forgive us our sins and purify us from all unrighteousness. If we claim we have not sinned, we make him out to be a liar and his word is not in us.'

Bible book

2 Corinthians

Date

Around AD 55

Author and target audience

2 Corinthians is basically the second part of 1 Corinthians, but in addition to still encouraging and shaping the Church, Paul brings in some helpful ideas and theologies.

Themes

Paul talks about God as Father, creator, and the One who raises Jesus from death. Paul also looks at Jesus and the Holy Spirit in helpful ways, and he speaks a bit about Satan too.

Verses

2 Corinthians 5:12-21

'We are not trying to commend ourselves to you again, but are giving you an opportunity to take pride in us, so that you can answer those who take pride in what is seen rather than in what is in the heart. If we are "out of our mind," as some say, it is for God; if we are in our right mind, it is for you. For Christ's love compels us, because we are convinced that one died for all, and therefore all died. And he died for all, that those who live should no longer live for themselves but for him who died for them and was raised again.

So from now on we regard no one from a worldly point of view. Though we once regarded Christ in this way, we do so no longer. Therefore, if anyone is in Christ, the new creation has come: the old has gone, the new is here! All this is from God, who reconciled us to himself through Christ and gave us the ministry of reconciliation: that God was reconciling the world to himself in Christ, not counting people's sins against them. And he has committed to us the message of reconciliation. We are therefore Christ's ambassadors, as though God were making his appeal through us. We implore you on Christ's behalf: be reconciled to God. God made him who had no sin to be sin for us, so that in him we might become the righteousness of God.'

The Questions

Explore

What stood out for you when you were reading these Bible verses?

cor. What do you think the apostle's when

        ministry was?

Jen: What was the same thing

        spiritual darkness without knowing

Did any particular sentences or individual words hit you or raise some questions? If so, what were they?

_____

_____

_____

Did you get any answers?

_____

_____

_____

Identify

What did you see in the verses that helped you see more of what forgiveness really means?

_____

_____

_____

What does the forgiveness of Jesus mean to you?

_____

_____

_____

What might the Holy Spirit be saying about something specific in your life today?

_____

_____

_____

Commit

How can you see this applying to your life?

_____

_____

_____

What can you put in place this week or month that will build on this revelation/discovery?

_____

_____

_____

What do you need to be accountable for at the moment?

_____

_____

_____

Don't let it drift to nothing – commit it to prayer and be accountable to update on it next session. You might like to write down some prayer and/or action points to remember.

 **Bible Study 4:**
Love

Bible Book
John

Date
About AD 80-90

Author and target audience
This fourth Gospel was written by the apostle John, who was a disciple and friend of Jesus. John was aware of the other Gospel accounts of Matthew, Mark and Luke, and with that in mind he wrote and added his own experience and eye witness accounts of the life, death and resurrection of Jesus.

Themes
John's Gospel is basically summed up in one pivotal, evangelistic verse found in John 20:31. Go and have a look at it. The book of John is all about Jesus, His work, life, death and resurrection. John particularly pulls out signs that point to who Jesus is - the Son of God. When reading John, keep an eye out for words like: light, dark, love, hate, life, death, and see if you can find the seven 'I am' sayings of Jesus.

Verses

John 13:1-20

'It was just before the Passover Festival. Jesus knew that the hour had come for him to leave this world and go to the Father. Having loved his own who were in the world, he loved them to the end.

The evening meal was in progress, and the devil had already prompted Judas, the son of Simon Iscariot, to betray Jesus. Jesus knew that the Father had put all things under his power, and that he had come from God and was returning to God; so he got up from the meal, took off his outer clothing, and wrapped a towel round his waist. After that, he poured water into a basin and began to wash his disciples' feet, drying them with the towel that was wrapped round him.

He came to Simon Peter, who said to him, "Lord, are you going to wash my feet?"

Jesus replied, "You do not realise now what I am doing, but later you will understand."

"No," said Peter, "you shall never wash my feet."

Jesus answered, "Unless I wash you, you have no part with me." -- *why Not?*

"Then, Lord," Simon Peter replied, "not just my feet but my hands and my head as well!"

Jesus answered, "Those who have had a bath need only to wash their feet; their whole body is clean. And you are clean, though not every one of you." For he knew who was going to betray him, and that was why he said not every one was clean.

When he had finished washing their feet, he put on his clothes and returned to his place. "Do you understand what I have done for you?" he asked them. "You call me 'Teacher' and 'Lord', and rightly so, for that is what I am. Now that I, your Lord and Teacher, have washed your feet, you also should wash one another's feet. I have set you an example that you should do as I have done for you. Very truly I tell you, no servant is greater than his master, nor is a messenger greater than the one who sent him. Now that you know these things, you will be blessed if you do them.

"I am not referring to all of you; I know those I have chosen. But this is to fulfil this passage of Scripture: 'He who shared my bread has turned against me.'

"I am telling you now before it happens, so that when it does happen you will believe that I am who I am. Very truly I tell you, whoever accepts anyone I send accepts me; and whoever accepts me accepts the one who sent me.'"

Bible book

1 Corinthians

Date

Around AD 55

Author and target audience

The apostle Paul, writing to a church in Corinth that he had founded on a missionary journey there (Acts 18:1). Paul was helped by two Jewish believers, Priscilla and Aquila. He was also joined by Silas and Timothy, and preached in the synagogues there. The city had a lot going on, including about a thousand 'religious' prostitutes for the Greek goddess of love, Aphrodite. A challenging culture in which to share the cross of Jesus!

Themes

Part of Paul's letter to the church here is to outline the right teaching and structure for this new collection of Christians. He dealt with issues of disunity, sin in the church, marriage, worship, roles of men and women, spiritual gifts and more.

Verses

1 Corinthians 13:1-13

'If I speak in the tongues of men or of angels, but do not have love, I am only a resounding gong or a clanging cymbal. If I have the gift of prophecy and can fathom all mysteries and all knowledge, and if I have a faith that can move mountains, but do not have love, I am nothing. If I give all I possess to the poor and give over my body to hardship that I may boast, but do not have love, I gain nothing.

Love is patient, love is kind. It does not envy, it does not boast, it is not proud. It does not dishonour others, it is not self-seeking, it is not easily angered, it keeps no record of wrongs. Love does not delight in evil but rejoices with the truth. It always protects, always trusts, always hopes, always perseveres.

Love never fails. But where there are prophecies, they will cease; where there are tongues, they will be stilled; where there is knowledge, it will pass away. For we know in part and we prophesy in part, but when completeness comes, what is in part disappears. When I was a child, I talked like a child, I thought like a child, I reasoned like a child. When I became a man, I put the ways of childhood behind me. For now we see only a reflection as in a mirror; then we shall see face to face. Now I know in part; then I shall know fully, even as I am fully known.

And now these three remain: faith, hope and love. But the greatest of these is love.'

 # The Questions

Explore

What stood out for you when you were reading these Bible verses?

_____

_____

_____

Did any particular sentences or individual words hit you or raise some questions? If so, what were they?

_____

_____

_____

Did you get any answers?

_____

_____

_____

Identify

What did you see in the verses that helped you see more of Jesus and His love for you?

___

___

___

What does Christian love mean to you?

___

___

___

What might the Holy Spirit be saying about something specific in your life today?

___

___

___

1- Jesus Gave us an example, but what must we do.

- Cor. Was Paul challenging Aphrodite's interpretation of Love?

Commit

How can you see this applying to your life?

_____

_____

_____

What can you put in place this week or month that will build on this revelation/discovery?

_____

_____

_____

What do you need to be accountable for at the moment?

_____

_____

_____

Don't let it drift to nothing – commit it to prayer and be accountable to update on it next session. You might like to write down some prayer and/or action points to remember.

The last word

Let me finish off this book with a story which, to be honest, sums up what it's all been about.

I sent a copy of this manuscript to a great friend, Lyndon Bowring. Not only is Lyndon one of the calmest and humblest men I know, he is one of the most spirit-filled too. I asked him to have a read and let me know what he thought.

I was sitting at home on the sofa – I had two of my children fighting over what they wanted to watch on the TV, and my third child was using permanent marker pens on the table to colour with and tattoo her face. It was chaos. Then the phone rang.

It was Lyndon. He was calm, encouraging and had some feedback about this book. I tried to run into another room to give the impression that all was under control (don't we all try to pretend we lead perfect, straightforward lives from time to time?), but I think he could hear the tempest I was surrounded by.

Now here is the best bit. Lyndon responded to me with a verse from the Bible and it was this one: 'And the things you have heard me say in the presence of many witnesses entrust to reliable people who will also be qualified to teach others' (2 Tim. 2:2).

This was it! I grabbed a sticky note and scribbled it down so I wouldn't forget it. (I did forget, because I lost the sticky note and had to email Lyndon to get it again... but the main thing was – this was it!)

The generation of men who we can impact, build up, encourage and set loose to be kingdom radicals, like gospel commandos, is incredible. We can give ourselves to something many men before us have done. We can witness and build the gospel – the truth of Jesus – into the lives of other men and in our lives at the same time!

Lyndon had not only helped me finish this book, but he had done exactly what this book is about. He had invested in me, given me wisdom, and directed me to God's Word (the other thing I know is that this man prays for me and my family every day, but that's another book).

That's it, fellas, The challenge, adventure and fight is on for us to be these iron men! Not men hiding our weakness and sitting behind a false veneer of masculinity – 'Ugg – me show no pain!' – but men who have really yielded to the Holy Spirit; men who are shepherd warriors, ready to pay the cost and be forged in the process of building gospel men.

Are you ready and willing to be that sort of iron man? Good, now go and find your Timothy.

More good reads for men

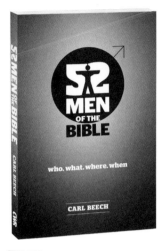 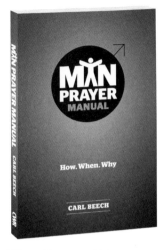

52 Men of the Bible
Who. What. Where. When

Dig deeper into the lives of some of the men in the Bible. From Adam to Jesus, explore how their example can affect your walk with God.

Author: Carl Beech
ISBN: 978-1-78259-154-2

Also available in eBook format

Man Prayer Manual
How. When. Why

Consider real-life stories of prayer and breakthrough, and be encouraged to live a dynamic life of prayer.

Author: Carl Beech
ISBN: 978-1-78259-522-9